COME SEE THE EARTH TURN

The Story of LÉON FOUCAULT

COME SEE THE EARTH TURN

The Story of
LÉON FOUCAULT

by LORI MORTENSEN · Illustrations by RAÚL ALLÉN

TRICYCLE PRESS
Berkeley

One ordinary autumn day, September 18, 1819, a baby was born in Paris, France.

He wasn't like other babies.

Instead of being fat and hearty, he was thin and weak.

Instead of a normal-sized head, his head was too small.

Instead of peering straight into his parents' eyes, his eyes looked away.

Each day his mama worried— would the baby live?

But day by day, the baby survived.

His parents named him Jean Bernard Léon Foucault.

PRONUNCIATION GUIDE

Jean Bernard Léon Foucault:
 zhon behr-NAR leh-ON foo-KO

Daguerreotype: da-GA-ree-o-TI-pe

Professor Donné: DOH-neh

Léon grew into a shy and awkward boy who often sat in a corner reading by himself.

At school, he was a tortoise among jackrabbits. Léon answered questions too slowly. He moved too slowly. And he was so slow finishing his homework that most of the time it was late.

His teachers shook their heads. What was wrong with the boy, anyway?

Léon passed his classes only with the help of his devoted mama.

Then Léon discovered that he had a talent for building things.

First he made a model boat, and then an optical telegraph just like the one on top of the neighboring Saint Sulpice Church.

Even though Léon's slowpoke ways got him in trouble at school, working slowly and precisely at home allowed him to make things exactly the way he wanted them to be.

Soon, family and friends marveled over the quiet boy's clever inventions and magnificent contraptions.

When Léon finished secondary school, his mama insisted that there was only one career for someone with such gifted hands. He would become a surgeon!

In 1839, his mama enrolled him in the Paris Medical School.

But the sight of suffering people and blood made him so sick he couldn't do his work. Léon had to leave medical school.

He would never be a surgeon.

However, one of his teachers was so impressed by his talent with instruments that he made Léon an assistant in his microscope class.

Léon stopped thinking about medicine and began thinking about science.

Before leaving school, Léon had discovered the work
of Louis-Jacques Daguerre, who invented an early form of
photography called the daguerreotype. As Léon worked
with gas-lit microscopes and studied how cameras worked,
he strived to answer larger questions about light—the
same questions asked by scientists at the nearby Academy
of Science:

What is the nature of light?
How fast does it travel?
How can such things be proved?

Over the next few years, Léon took the first photograph
of the sun, and measured the speed of light more accurately
than anyone before him.

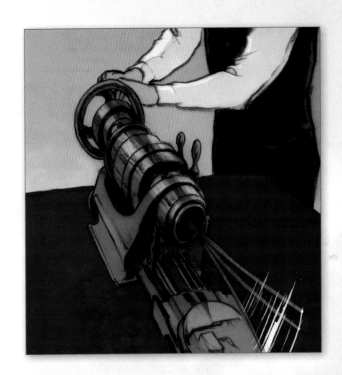

Then, one day, Léon made a startling discovery in his laboratory. He had clamped a steel rod into a lathe, a machine that allowed him to spin and shape objects. In moving around the machine, Léon accidentally twanged the tip of the rod, setting it wiggling from side to side. Léon slowly turned the machine's crank to start the rod spinning. To his amazement, he saw that even though the rod began to spin, the tip kept wiggling side to side, independently from the spinning motion.

At that moment, Léon understood how to answer a question that had baffled scientists for centuries: how can science prove that the earth spins on its axis?

It was no idle question. Two centuries earlier, church leaders in Rome had declared that the earth was the unmoving center of the universe. People who challenged the church on this matter were imprisoned, tortured, or killed as heretics.

By the nineteenth century, church leaders and scientists had learned more about the universe. Now, almost everyone believed that the earth did indeed turn, but no one had been able to *prove* that it did.

Some said it was impossible.

In 1638, a monk and his assistant tried to prove that the earth turned by blasting a cannonball straight up into the sky.

They never saw the cannonball again.

Others dropped lead balls from high towers or down deep mine shafts.

Each experiment tried to show that if the earth were rotating, the ball would land in a different spot from where it had been launched.

However, wind, temperature, and mistakes in measurement made it impossible for the scientists to prove anything.

But when Léon saw the spinning rod, he knew the answer: a pendulum.

Like the rod, a pendulum could move independently from an object turning beneath it.

To prove his idea, Léon worked feverishly with weights, wires, and brass bobs in the cold, damp cellar of his home.

One of his biggest challenges was designing a device that would suspend the pendulum but also allow it to swing freely, without interfering with its movement.

Another challenge was simply finding a quiet place to work. Carriages rumbled down the street, blacksmiths hammered, and steam engines pounded. All these vibrations ruined Léon's careful measurements.

So Léon often worked while the rest of Paris slept.

Finally, on a cold, quiet, winter night, Léon released his pendulum. A long wire, suspended by a device he had designed, swept a heavy brass bob across the cellar.

Léon watched and waited.

Then he saw it—something no one else in the world had ever seen.

Wednesday, January 8, 2am:

The pendulum turned

Three weeks later, the scientific community in Paris received handwritten cards.

On February 3, 1851, scientists from all over Paris gathered in Meridian Hall, where a line called the Paris Meridian was traced in the floor, running precisely from north to south.

The distinguished crowd watched as Léon burned a woolen thread so the pendulum would not be influenced by his touch. The thread smoldered, then snapped, releasing the brass pendulum across the room.

The great bob swung back and forth along the line etched in the floor.

Swish.

Swish.

Swish.

What would they see?
The crowd watched and waited.
Minutes passed. . . .
Would anything happen?

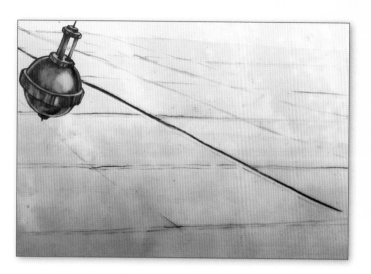

Then they saw it—the pendulum began swinging away from the line traced in the floor.

In an instant, the scientists knew: The pendulum wasn't swinging in a different direction. The earth was rotating beneath it.

Léon Foucault, the frail, awkward boy, had proved that the earth turned.

AUTHOR'S NOTE

Léon Foucault's experiment was so amazing yet so simple that many called it Foucault's *belle expérience* or "beautiful experiment." It didn't take long for "pendulum mania" to spread around the world. "The experiment excited the astonishment of every beholder," wrote one *Times* journalist, "and many eminent scientific gentlemen who were present expressed their great delight in witnessing a phenomenon which they considered the most satisfactory they had witnessed in the whole course of their lives."

But because Léon Foucault was not a trained scientist with an academic pedigree, many of Paris's elite scientists were resentful of his spectacular success. Mathematicians and physicists wondered why their calculations hadn't predicted the answer. Léon's experiment was so simple—why hadn't *they* thought of it? To protect themselves from looking bad, many scrambled through old calculations and scientific papers to show that the seeds of the idea were there all along.

While Léon received honors for his pendulum and for his achievements with light, telescopes, and photography from Napoléon the Third and many foreign countries, he was not granted membership into France's exclusive Academy of Science until three years before his death. Without a degree in physics or mathematics, his application for membership had been regularly rejected. He later said that his membership in the Academy was one of the joys of his life.

In July 1867, Léon's health began to fail. During the next six months, paralysis spread through his body, affecting his ability to walk, see, and speak. Although no one knows exactly what illness he had, experts believe he suffered from rapid onset of multiple sclerosis, a disease of the nervous system. Léon Foucault died on February 11, 1868, at the age of forty-eight in the home he shared with his mother.

GLOSSARY

lathe: a machine used for shaping materials such as wood, steel, glass, and clay. As the lathe spins the material around its axis, the operator applies a cutting or shaping tool against the material, carving it into a new shape.

microscope: an instrument that uses lenses to magnify images of objects that often cannot be seen by the human eye.

optical telegraph: a device used to send and receive visual messages over long distances. In France between 1792 and 1846, optical telegraphs were shaped like a giant capital letter *T* and built on towers about twenty miles apart. Operators moved paddles at the end of the "arms" to form different letters. They could send about two words per minute.

pendulum: a weight or "bob" that swings back and forth while suspended from a fixed point. Pendulums are often used in clocks, and you might even find one on the playground—swings!

"The pendulum turned...": Léon's actual words were, "The pendulum turned in the direction of the diurnal motion of the celestial sphere." What did he mean? He meant that the pendulum was turning in the same direction that the stars and planets appeared to be turning in the sky.

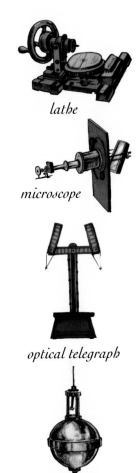

lathe

microscope

optical telegraph

pendulum

BIBLIOGRAPHY

1. Aczel, Amir D. *Pendulum of Léon Foucault and the Triumph of Science.* New York: Atria Books, 2003.

2. Cunningham, Clifford J. "How Do We Know Earth Rotates?" *Mercury* 31, no. 4 (July/August 2002): 13.

3. Huges, David. "King of the Swingers." *New Scientist* 180, no. 2426-2428 (December 20, 2003): 82.

4. Thomas, Isabel. *The Day the Earth Stood Still: Earth's Movement in Space.* Bloomington: Raintree Press, 2005.

5. Tobin, William. *The Life and Science of Léon Foucault – The Man Who Proved the Earth Rotates.* Cambridge: Cambridge University Press, 2003.

6. Tobin, William. "Leon Foucault." *Scientific American* 279, no. 1, U.S. edition (July 1998): 70.

7. PBS Kids. "Pendulum: Make It Swing!"
   http://pbskids.org/zoom/games/pendulum/foucault.html

8. Arts et Metiers Museum. "The Foucault's Pendulum of the 'Arts et Metiers' Museum from Paris."
   http://visite.artsetmetiers.free.fr/site_anglais/pendulum_museum_a.html

9. Center for Science and Industry. "Foucault's Pendulum."
   http://www.cosi.org/visitors/exhibits/hallway/pendulum/

To Dad, who taught me how to make quantitative transfers. —L.M.

To my family for helping me become what I am now, to Jenny for helping me see Leòn, to Borja Pindado for his aid with the color, to Abigail for pushing all limits known to man, and to Raquel for everything. —R.A.

All rights reserved. Published in the United States by Tricycle Press, an imprint of Random House Children's Books,
a division of Random House, Inc., New York.
www.randomhouse.com/kids

Tricycle Press and the Tricycle Press colophon are
registered trademarks of Random House, Inc.

Library of Congress Cataloging-in-Publication Data

Mortensen, Lori, 1955-
Come See the Earth Turn : The Story of Léon Foucault / by Lori Mortensen ; illustrations by Raúl Allén.
p. cm.
ISBN-13: 978-1-58246-284-4 (hardcover)
ISBN-10: 1-58246-284-4 (hardcover)
1. Foucault's pendulum—Juvenile literature. 2. Earth—Rotation—Juvenile literature.
3. Foucault, Léon, 1819-1868—Juvenile literature.
4. Physicists—France—Biography—Juvenile literature. I. Allen, Raul, ill. II. Title.
QB633.M778 2010
525'.36—dc22

2009032301

ISBN 978-1-58246-284-4 (hardcover)
ISBN 978-1-58246-361-2 (Gibraltar lib. bdg.)

Printed in Malaysia

Design by Susan Van Horn
Typeset in Archive French Shaded, Pabst, Cochin, and P22 Declaration Alternate
The illustrations in this book were rendered in pencil and watercolor, and finished in Adobe Photoshop.

1 2 3 4 5 6 – 15 14 13 12 11 10

First Edition